CH

# VETERANS DAY

## ARLENE WORSLEY

www.av2books.com

**BOOK CODE**

P439570

**AV² by Weigl** brings you media enhanced books that support active learning.

AV² provides enriched content that supplements and complements this book. Weigl's AV² books strive to create inspired learning and engage young minds for a total learning experience.

Go to **www.av2books.com**, and enter this book's unique code. You will have access to video, audio, web links, quizzes, a slide show, and activities.

**Audio**
Listen to sections of the book read aloud.

**Video**
Watch informative video clips.

**Web Link**
Find research sites and play interactive games.

**Try This!**
Complete activities and hands-on experiments.

Due to the dynamic nature of the Internet, some of the URLs and activities provided as part of AV² by Weigl may have changed or ceased to exist. AV² by Weigl accepts no responsibility for any such changes. All media enhanced books are regularly monitored to update addresses and sites in a timely manner. Contact AV² by Weigl at 1-866-649-3445 or av2books@weigl.com with any questions, comments, or feedback.

Published by AV² By Weigl
350 5th Avenue, 59th Floor
New York, NY 10118
Website: www.av2books.com    www.weigl.com

Library of Congress Cataloging-in-Publication Data

Worsley, Arlene.
Veterans Day / Arlene Worsley.
     p. cm. -- (American celebrations)
Originally published: c2007.
Includes index.
ISBN 978-1-60596-774-5 (hardcover : alk. paper) -- ISBN 978-1-60596-932-9 (softcover : alk. paper) --
ISBN 978-1-60596-939-8 (e-book)
1.  Veterans Day--Juvenile literature.  I. Title.
D671.W67 2011
394.264--dc22
                              2009050992

Printed in the United States of America in North Mankato, Minnesota
1 2 3 4 5 6 7 8 9 0  14 13 12 11 10

**Editor**  Heather C. Hudak    **Design**  Terry Paulhus

052010
WEP264000

Every reasonable effort has been made to trace ownership and to obtain permission to reprint copyright material. The publishers would be pleased to have any errors or omissions brought to their attention so that they may be corrected in subsequent printings.

Weigl Publishers acknowledges Getty Images as its primary image supplier for this title.

# CONTENTS

# What is Veterans Day?

November 11 is **Veterans** Day. In 1918, it was the day a peace agreement was signed to end World War I. Veterans Day is observed every year in the United States. On this day, Americans honor war veterans who served in all wars. Americans also honor those who served on military missions to maintain peace in warring countries.

On Veterans Day, special events take place at war **memorials** across the United States. Veterans, soldiers, and citizens place flowers and flags on graves. Some people quietly pay their respects at private services. Veterans Day is a time to give thanks to all those who have served to protect America's freedom.

# Special Events
## THROUGHOUT THE YEAR

**JANUARY 1**
NEW YEAR'S DAY

**FEBRUARY (THIRD MONDAY)**
PRESIDENTS' DAY

**MARCH 17**
ST. PATRICK'S DAY

**SUNDAY IN MARCH OR APRIL**
EASTER

**MAY (LAST MONDAY)**
MEMORIAL DAY

**JUNE 14**
FLAG DAY

**JULY 4**
INDEPENDENCE DAY

**AUGUST (FIRST SUNDAY)**
FAMILY DAY

**SEPTEMBER (FIRST MONDAY)**
LABOR DAY

**OCTOBER (SECOND MONDAY)**
COLUMBUS DAY

 **NOVEMBER 11**
VETERANS DAY

**DECEMBER 25**
CHRISTMAS DAY

# Veterans Day History

**A** war broke out in Europe in 1914. This war involved almost every country in the world. It was called the Great War. Today, the Great War is known as World War I. The United States joined the war in 1917. Millions of Americans served in the war. Armed forces fought in trenches. These were forts dug deep into the ground. Trenches were one of the most dangerous points of combat.

✫✫ **More than 20,000 women took part in World War I. They belonged to the Army and Navy Nurse Corps, the Marine Corps, and the Coast Guard.**

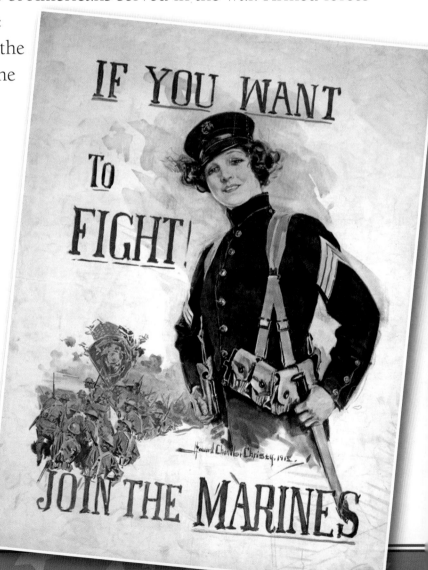

IF YOU WANT To FIGHT! JOIN THE MARINES

★ More than 116,000 American soldiers lost their lives in the Great War.

After four years, World War I came to a close on November 11, 1918. The Armistice Treaty was signed to end the war. This was a peace agreement between Germany and the **Allied Powers**. In the United States, many people lined the streets celebrating the victory. Americans danced and cheered as bells and whistles sounded. Businesses also closed for the day. Americans wanted to remember those who died in the war. Memorials were built in cities, towns, and villages. In 1919, President Woodrow Wilson named November 11 Armistice Day.

## Past and Present Celebrations

VETERANS DAY was originally observed as Armistice Day. The first event took place on November 11, 1919, and was honored with parades, public meetings, and a moment of silence. By 1926, 27 states had declared Armistice Day a legal holiday.

IN 1938, Armistice Day was made a national holiday. All states made November 11 a holiday so that most people could attend parades and ceremonies to honor fallen soldiers.

SINCE 1954, Americans have honored November 11 as Veterans Day. Today, there are still ceremonies and a moment of silence at 11 a.m. to remember those who died in service of peace.

# Important People

On January 8, 1918, President Woodrow Wilson gave an important speech to **Congress**. He outlined his goals to end the war. These became known as the Fourteen Points. President Wilson wanted cooperation from all countries involved. To achieve peace between nations, he encouraged freedom to cross the seas and to return **independence** to occupied lands. President Wilson also wanted to limit the use of weapons and maintain the right of independent countries to govern their own people.

President Wilson's Fourteen Points became the basis of Germany's **surrender** in November 1918. They also formed the foundation of the League of Nations, the world's first international peace organization.

★ President Wilson's quest for peace led to the creation of the League of Nations in 1919. This was an organization that promoted international cooperation. In 1946, the United Nations replaced the League of Nations.

President Woodrow Wilson offered these words about peace. "It is that the world be made fit and safe to live in; and particularly that it be made safe for every peace-loving nation which, like our own, wishes to live its own life,

⭐ **President Woodrow Wilson was awarded the Nobel Prize for Peace in 1919.**

determine its own institutions, be assured of justice and fair dealing by the other peoples of the world as against force and selfish aggression. All the peoples of the world are in effect partners in this interest, and for our own part we see very clearly that unless justice be done to others, it will not be done to us. The program of the world's peace, therefore, is our program."

# First-hand Account

"On this Veterans Day of 1961, on this day of remembrance, let us pray in the name of those who have fought in this country's wars, and most especially who have fought in the First World War and in the Second World War, that there will be no veterans of any further war—not because all shall have perished but because all shall have learned to live together in peace."

*This is part of a speech President John F. Kennedy gave on Veterans Day at **Arlington National Cemetery** in 1961.*

# Veterans Day Celebrations

From 1919 to 1954, November 11 was called Armistice Day. The United States Congress made Armistice Day a national holiday in 1938. Raymond Weeks, an American **patriot**, organized the first Armistice Day parade in 1947. It was held in Birmingham, Alabama. He wanted to honor "all of America's veterans for their loyal service."

President Dwight D. Eisenhower changed the name of the holiday to Veterans Day in 1954. Now, every year on the 11th hour, of the 11th day, of the 11th month, Americans remember their heroes of war and of peace.

⭐⭐ The Pacific Pavilion World War II memorial is found at the World War II Memorial in Washington, D.C.

Veterans Day is a day to remember war heroes from all wars. It is also a day to honor the brave military personnel who defend the United States today.

Many other countries have celebrations to honor veterans. Great Britain, Canada, and France remember their veterans on or around November 11. The dates are so close because each country's holiday was started to celebrate the end of World War I and the following peace.

# Ceremonies Around the World

## CANADA

Remembrance Day takes place on November 11. This is an annual holiday that honors the **sacrifices** members of the armed forces and civilians have made in times of war. During the weeks leading up to the day, poppies are sold to support veterans. Many people wear these poppy pins to show their support.

## GREAT BRITAIN

Armed Forces Day celebrates the service of men and women in the British Armed Forces. It was first celebrated in 2006 as Veterans' Day, but in 2009 the name was changed to Armed Forces Day to raise awareness of men and women still serving.

## FRANCE

Armistice Day is a public holiday in France. Since the Armistice Treaty was signed on November 11, 1918, the day has been a holiday. The French observe the day with a ceremony at the Arc de Triomphe, which holds the Tomb of the Unknown Soldier from World War I.

# Celebrating Today

On Veterans Day, cities and towns all over the country have parades and ceremonies. An important national ceremony is at the Tomb of the Unknowns in Arlington, Virginia.

During the ceremony, the president of the United States lays a wreath on the tomb. He then steps back and salutes. A bugler plays "Taps." This song is a farewell to those who died in war.

National Veterans Awareness Week is held one week before Veterans Day. Students learn about how veterans helped defend America's freedom.

★★ After the bugler plays "Taps," many veterans groups march in the Parade of Flags inside the Memorial Amphitheater.

Many states also have war memorials, such as the Vietnam Memorial on the grounds of the state capitol in Phoenix, Arizona.

# Veterans Day in the United States

Veterans Day is celebrated all over the United States. Many Americans visit war memorials and cemeteries. Veterans are also invited to local schools to talk about their war experience.

**CALIFORNIA** In San Francisco, California, there was a week-long Veterans Day celebration in 2000. Many people visited the Moving Wall. This is a traveling wall that contains engraved names of American soldiers who lost their lives in the Vietnam War. It is half the size of the war memorial in Washington, D.C.

**California**

**HAWAI'I** The annual Veterans Day ceremony in Honolulu, Hawai'i, is at the National Memorial Cemetery of the Pacific. Many people also visit the USS *Arizona* Memorial in Pearl Harbor. They remember the soldiers who defended America's freedom during World War II.

Hawai'i

0    970 Miles

Alaska

0    1,278 Miles

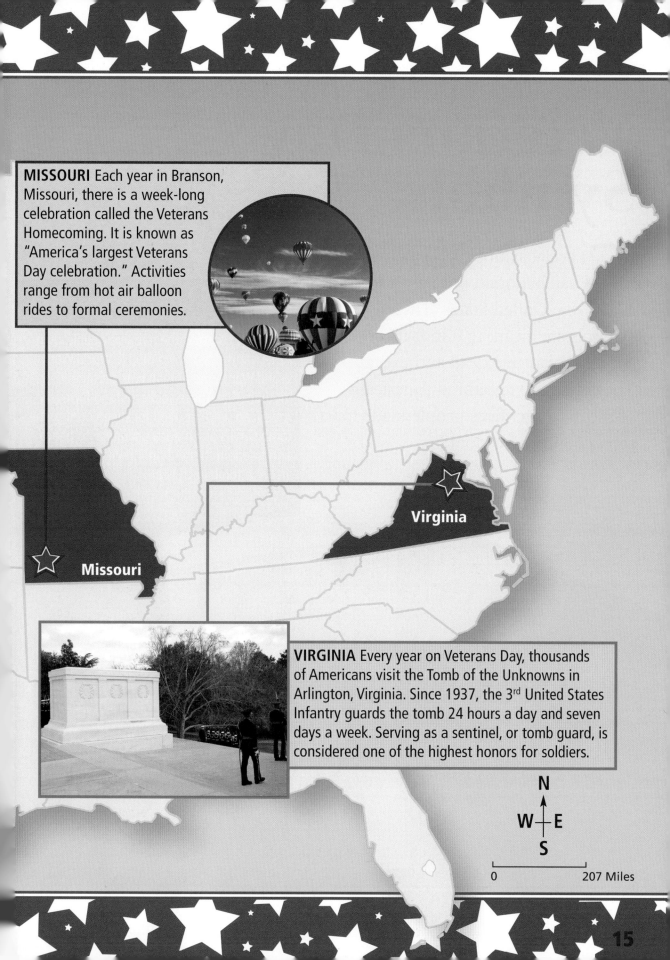

**MISSOURI** Each year in Branson, Missouri, there is a week-long celebration called the Veterans Homecoming. It is known as "America's largest Veterans Day celebration." Activities range from hot air balloon rides to formal ceremonies.

Virginia

Missouri

**VIRGINIA** Every year on Veterans Day, thousands of Americans visit the Tomb of the Unknowns in Arlington, Virginia. Since 1937, the 3rd United States Infantry guards the tomb 24 hours a day and seven days a week. Serving as a sentinel, or tomb guard, is considered one of the highest honors for soldiers.

N
W E
S

0          207 Miles

# Veterans Day Symbols

Special symbols of remembrance can be found in many parts of the United States. These symbols are meant to honor the country's wartime dead and living. They also help to remind Americans of the great sacrifices people made for their country's freedom.

## TOMB OF THE UNKNOWNS

The tomb contains the remains of unknown American soldiers who died in World War I, World War II, the Korean War, and the Vietnam War. These soldiers stand for every American who has died for their country. The tomb serves as America's promise to peace and freedom. More than 4 million Americans visit the tomb each year.

## POPPIES

After World War I, an American named Moina Michael began selling paper poppies. The money she raised was used to support war veterans. The poppy became an official memorial flower in 1922. Americans wear poppies on their coats and hats to honor those who served the United States in war and in peace.

## MEMORIALS

One of the most important memorials is the United States Marine Corps Memorial. It is located in Washington, D.C. The statue shows the raising of the United States flag atop Mount Suribachi in Japan during World War II. It is dedicated to the U.S. Marine Corps, who have defended the United States since 1775.

# A Poem to Remember

"A Nation's Strength" is a poem by Ralph Waldo Emerson. It says that the strength of a nation comes from the people who live there.

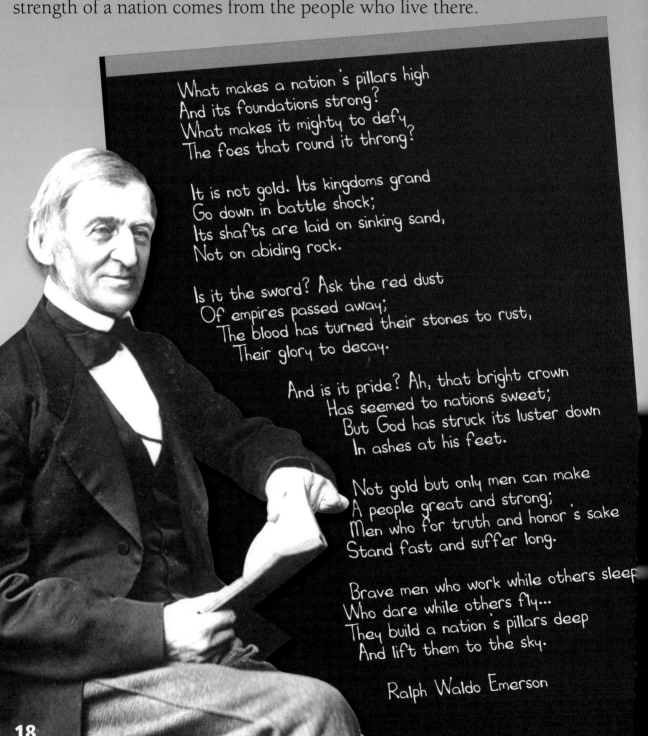

What makes a nation's pillars high
And its foundations strong?
What makes it mighty to defy
The foes that round it throng?

It is not gold. Its kingdoms grand
Go down in battle shock;
Its shafts are laid on sinking sand,
Not on abiding rock.

Is it the sword? Ask the red dust
Of empires passed away;
The blood has turned their stones to rust,
Their glory to decay.

And is it pride? Ah, that bright crown
Has seemed to nations sweet;
But God has struck its luster down
In ashes at his feet.

Not gold but only men can make
A people great and strong;
Men who for truth and honor's sake
Stand fast and suffer long.

Brave men who work while others sleep
Who dare while others fly...
They build a nation's pillars deep
And lift them to the sky.

Ralph Waldo Emerson

# Write Your Own Poem

Writing a poem is one way people record their feelings and opinions. Many people write poems because it helps them express their thoughts. Follow these steps to write your own poem.

Some poems rhyme. Others follow a special format. Choose a style for your poem.

Select a topic for your poem. Write about a subject you know well, such as your feelings or a place you have visited.

Word choice is important when writing poems. Use precise words and details. Proper word selection is essential for a strong poem.

Write about personal experiences. This will help paint a picture for people reading your poem.

Use the five senses to help you describe your thoughts.

Share your poem with friends. Ask them to provide feedback about how your poem made them feel. What can you do to improve your writing?

# Writing a Thank You Card

Thank you cards are a great way to let local war veterans know how much you appreciate them.

Construction paper

Pen, marker, or pencil

Envelope

Stamps

## 4 Easy Steps to Complete Your Centerpiece

**1** To begin, fold a piece of construction paper in half. Now, you have the base for your card.

**2** On the front of the card, draw a picture that shows your feelings about Veterans Day.

**3** On the inside of the card, write a thank you message or a poem about war and peace.

**4** Send the card to your local branch of the American Legion, or ask your parents to help you deliver it in person.

# Berry Shortcake

**Ingredients**

6 cups of berries
8 ready-made English biscuits
1 cup of ready-made whipped cream
4 tablespoons of sugar

**Equipment**

large bowl
whisk
8 saucer plates

**Direction**

1. Wash the berries, and place them in a large bowl.
2. Sprinkle sugar over the berries, and gently stir with a tablespoon.
3. On each saucer plate, add 2 tablespoons of berries. Scoop one heaping tablespoon of whipped cream on the center of the berries.
4. Place one ready-made biscuit on top of the whipped cream on each plate.
5. Add 1 tablespoon of berries to the top of each biscuit. Then, scoop 1 tablespoon of whipped cream on top of the berries.
6. Top each shortcake with one berry, and serve to family and friends.

yummy!

# Test Your Knowledge!

**1**

Where is the Tomb of the Unkowns?

**2**

At what time on Veterans Day do Americans have a moment of silence?

**3**

What instrument is "Taps" usually played on?

**4**

Which war is known as the Great War?

**5**

What was Veterans Day originally called?

**Quiz Answers:**
1. The Tomb of the Unkowns is at Arlington, Virginia.
2. Americans have a moment of silence at 11:00 a.m. on Veterans Day.
3. "Taps" is played on a bugle.
4. The Great War is also known as World War I.
5. Veterans Day was first called Armistice Day.

# Glossary

**Allied Powers:** a military partnership during World War I consisting of 28 countries in opposition to another group of countries

**Arlington National Cemetery:** one of the largest cemeteries in the United States; located in Virginia, most of the people who died during Civil War battle are buried here

**Congress:** a governing body of the United States

**independence:** freedom from control

**memorials:** places where people who have died are laid to rest

**patriot:** a person who loves and supports the country in which he or she lives

**sacrifices:** valuable things given up for a special cause

**surrender:** to declare defeat

**veterans:** people who have served in war

# Index

# Log on to www.av2books.com

AV² by Weigl brings you media enhanced books that support active learning. Go to **www.av2books.com**, and enter the special code inside the front cover of this book. You will gain access to enriched and enhanced content that supplements and complements this book. Content includes video, audio, web links, quizzes, a slide show, and activities.

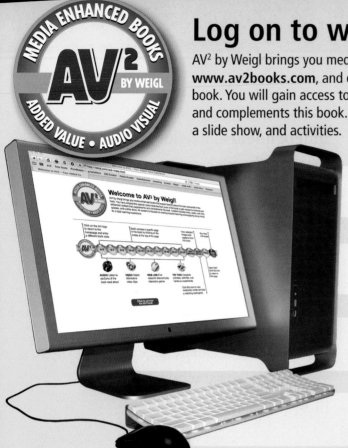

**Audio**
Listen to sections of the book read aloud.

**Video**
Watch informative video clips.

**Web Link**
Find research sites and play interactive games.

**Try This!**
Complete activities and hands-on experiments.

# WHAT'S ONLINE?

|  **Try This!** Complete activities and hands-on experiments. |  **Web Link** Find research sites and play interactive games. |  **Video** Watch informative video clips. | **EXTRA FEATURES** |
|---|---|---|---|
| **Pages 8-9** Write a biography about an important person | **Pages 6-7** Find out more about the history of Veterans Day | **Pages 4-5** Watch a video about Veterans Day |  **Audio** Hear introductory a at the top of every p |
| **Pages 10-11** Describe the features and special events of a similar celebration around the world | **Pages 10-11** Learn more about similar celebrations around the world | **Pages 12-13** Check out a video about how people celebrate Veterans Day | **Key Words** Study vocabulary, and play a matching word game. |
| **Pages 14-15** Complete a mapping activity about Veterans Day celebrations | **Pages 16-17** Find information about important holiday symbols | | **Slide Show** View images and captions, and try a writing activity. |
| **Pages 16-17** Try this activity about important holiday symbols | **Pages 18-19** Link to more information about Veterans Day | | **AV² Quiz** Take this quiz to test your knowledge |
| **Pages 20-21** Play an interactive activity | **Pages 20-21** Check out more holiday craft ideas | | |